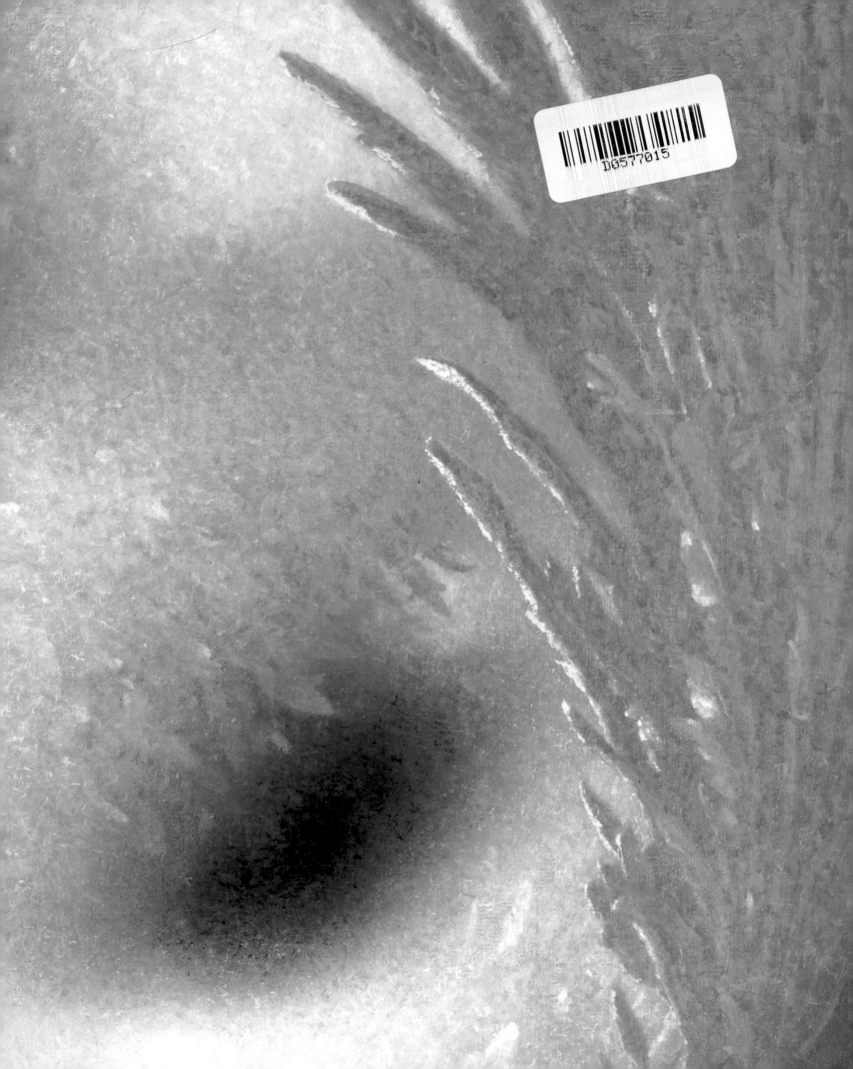

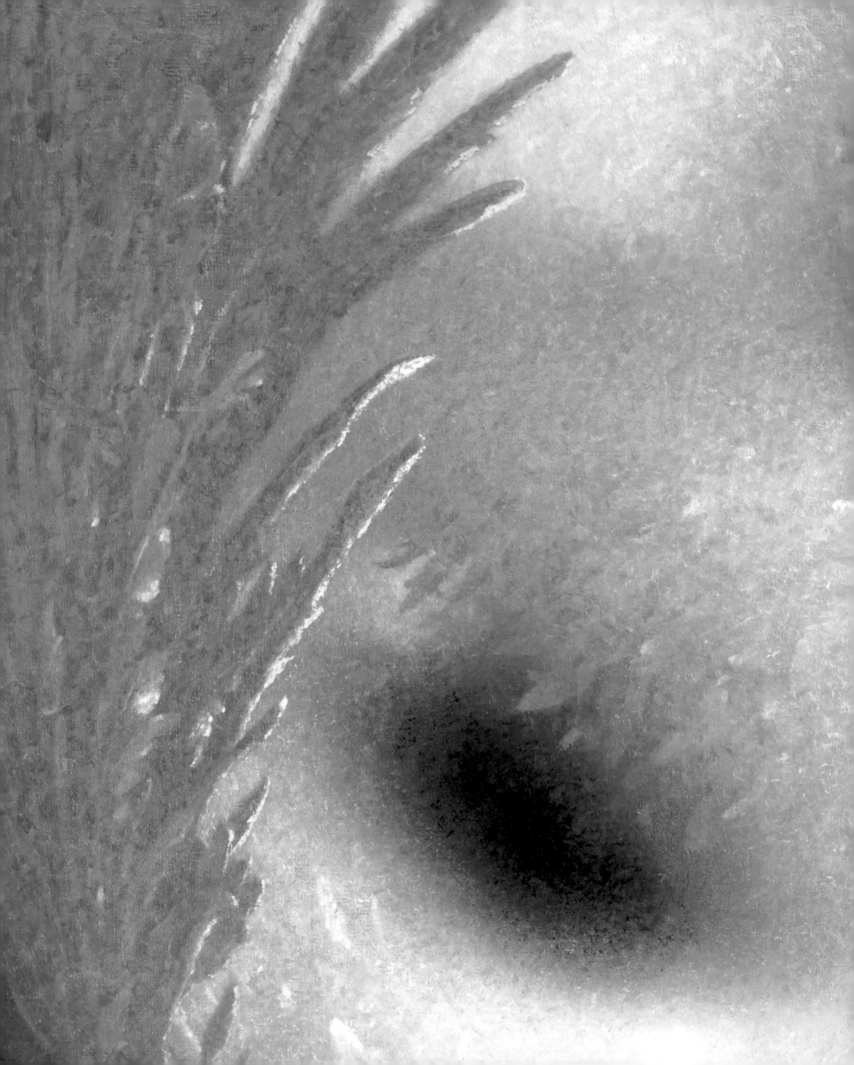

This Is the Star

For the newly born.
J.D.

To Lin.
G.B.

This Is the Star

JOYCE DUNBAR ✦ GARY BLYTHE

HARCOURT BRACE & COMPANY
San Diego   New York   London

This is the star in the sky.

These are the shepherds watching by night
That saw the star in the sky.

This is the angel shining bright
Who came to the shepherds watching by night
That saw the star in the sky.

This is the donkey with precious load
Trudging the long and weary road,
Looked on by the angel shining bright
Who came to the shepherds watching by night
That saw the star in the sky.

This is the inn where the only room
Was a stable out in the lamplit gloom
For the donkey and his precious load
Who trudged the long and weary road,
Looked on by the angel shining bright
Who came to the shepherds watching by night
That saw the star in the sky.

This is the ox and this is the ass
Who saw such wonders come to pass
At the darkened inn where the only room
Was a stable out in the lamplit gloom
For the donkey and his precious load
Who trudged the long and weary road,
Looked on by the angel shining bright
Who came to the shepherds watching by night
That saw the star in the sky.

This is the manger warm with hay
Wherein a newborn baby lay.
This is the ox and this the ass
Who saw these wonders come to pass
At the darkened inn where the only room
Was a stable out in the lamplit gloom
For the donkey and his precious load
Who trudged the long and weary road,
Looked on by the angel shining bright
Who came to the shepherds watching by night
That saw the star in the sky.

This is the gold and fragrant myrrh
And frankincense, the gifts that were
Placed by the manger warm with hay
Wherein a newborn baby lay.
This is the ox and this the ass
Who saw these wonders come to pass
At the darkened inn where the only room
Was a stable out in the lamplit gloom
For the donkey and his precious load
Who trudged the long and weary road,
Looked on by the angel shining bright
Who came to the shepherds watching by night
That saw the star in the sky.

These are the wise men come from afar
Who also saw and followed the star,
Bearing the gold and fragrant myrrh
And frankincense, the gifts that were
Placed by the manger warm with hay
Wherein a newborn baby lay.
This is the ox and this the ass
Who saw these wonders come to pass
At the darkened inn where the only room
Was a stable out in the lamplit gloom
For the donkey and his precious load
Who trudged the long and weary road,
Looked on by the angel shining bright
Who came to the shepherds watching by night
That saw the star in the sky.

This is the child that was born.

This is the Christ child born to be king
While hosts of heavenly angels sing.
These are the wise men come from afar
Who also saw and followed the star,
Bearing the gold and fragrant myrrh
And frankincense, the gifts that were
Placed by the manger warm with hay
Wherein a newborn baby lay.
This is the ox and this the ass
Who saw these wonders come to pass
At the darkened inn where the only room
Was a stable out in the lamplit gloom
For the donkey and his precious load
Who trudged the long and weary road,
Looked on by the angel shining bright
Who came to the shepherds watching by night
That saw the star in the sky.

Still shines the star in the sky.

First U.S. edition 1996
First published in Great Britain in 1996 by Transworld Publishers Ltd.

Library of Congress Cataloging-in-Publication Data
Dunbar, Joyce.
This is the star/Joyce Dunbar; illustrated by Gary Blythe.
p. cm.
Summary: A cumulative presentation which uses rhyme
to describe the night of the birth of Christ.
ISBN 0-15-200851-9
1. Jesus Christ—Nativity—Juvenile literature.
{1. Jesus Christ—Nativity. 2. Christmas.} I. Blythe, Gary, ill.
II. Title.
BT315.2.D86 1996
232.92—dc20 95-50730

Printed in Belgium by Proost

A C E F D B

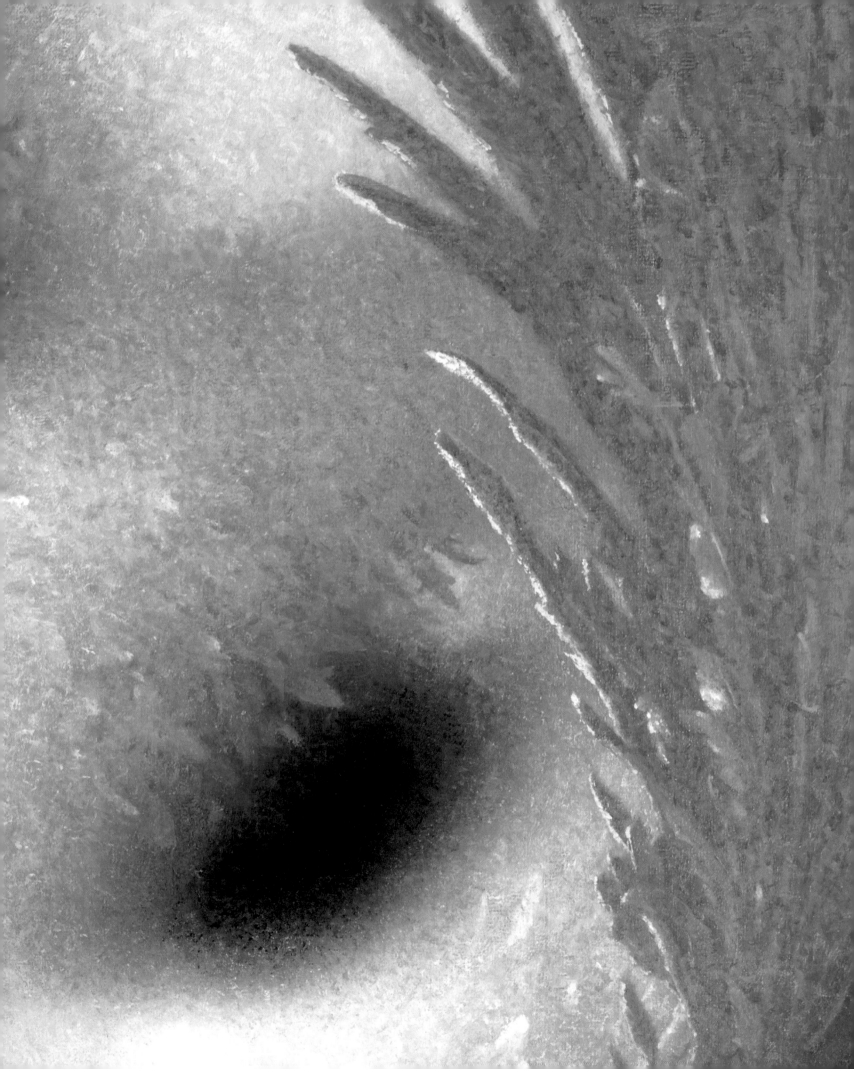

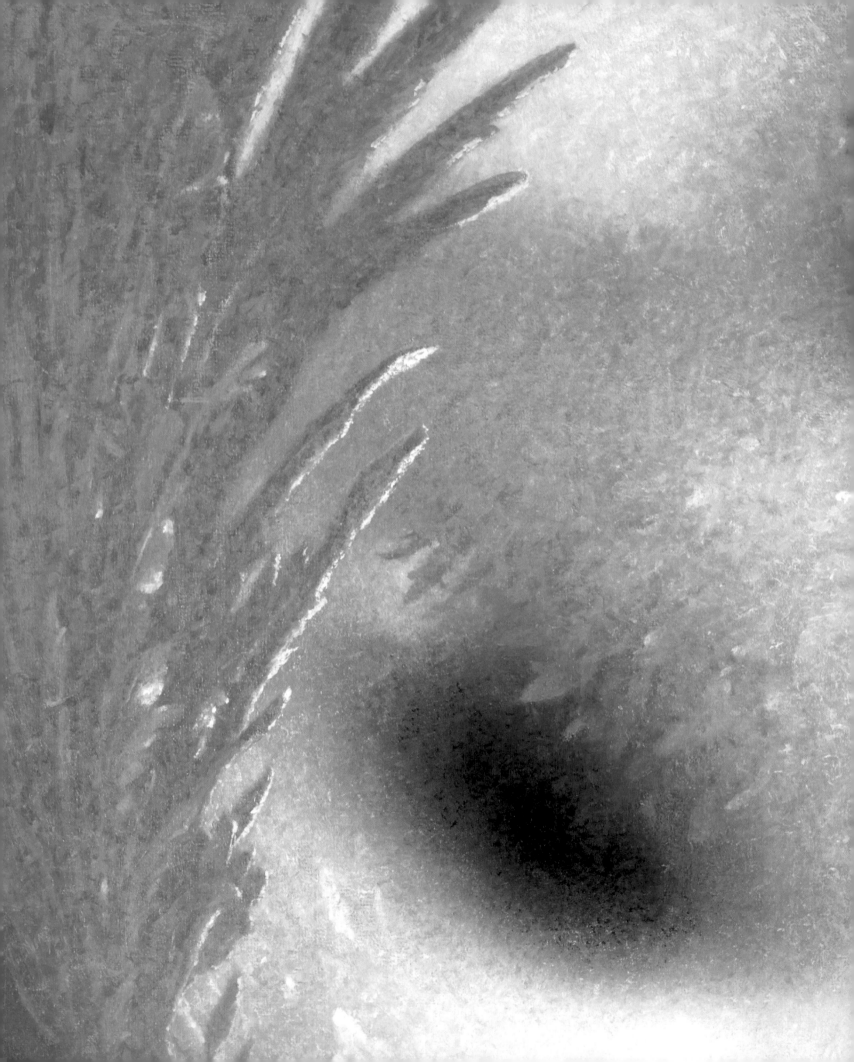